A DESERT
FOOD CHAIN

A DESERT FOOD CHAIN

ODYSSEYS

A. D. TARBOX

CREATIVE EDUCATION•CREATIVE PAPERBACKS

Published by Creative Education and Creative Paperbacks
P.O. Box 227, Mankato, Minnesota 56002
Creative Education and Creative Paperbacks
are imprints of The Creative Company
www.thecreativecompany.us

Design and production by Blue Design
Art direction by Rita Marshall
Printed in the United States of America

Photographs by Alamy (Danita Delimont, franzfoto.com, Ron
Niebrugge), Corbis (Michael & Patricia Fogden, Kevin Schafer,
Kennan Ward), Getty Images (Altrendo Nature, Tom Bean,
Walter Bibikow, James P. Blair, Jonathan Blair, Rosemary
Calvert, Tim Fitzharris, Tim Flach, Jeff Foott, Wyatt Gallery,
Patricio Robles Gil/Sierra Madre, Tim Graham, Gavin Hellier,
Mattias Klum/National Geographic, Mark Moffett, Marc
Moritsch, Klaus Nigge, Tom Vezo)

Library of Congress Cataloging-in-Publication Data
Tarbox, A. D. (Angelique D.)
A desert food chain / A. D. Tarbox.
p. cm. — (Odysseys in nature)
Summary: A look at a common food chain in a North
American desert, introducing the mesquite tree that starts the
chain, the coyote that sits atop the chain, and various animals
in between.
Includes bibliographical references and index.
ISBN 978-1-60818-539-9 (hardcover)
ISBN 978-1-62832-140-1 (pbk)
1. Desert ecology—Southwest, New—Juvenile literature. 2.
Food chains (Ecology)—Southwest, New—Juvenile literature.
3. Southwest, New—Juvenile literature. I. Title.

QH541.5.D4T37 2015
577.54—dc23   2014038227

CCSS: RI.8.1, 2, 3, 4; RI.9-10.1, 2, 3, 4; RI.11-12.1, 2, 3, 4

First Edition HC 9 8 7 6 5 4 3 2 1
First Edition PBK 9 8 7 6 5 4 3 2 1

Cover: A camel
Page 2: A coyote
Pages 4–5: A lappet-faced vulture
Page 6: Desert sands near a mountain range

CONTENTS

Introduction

A bird swoops through the sky. In the depths of the sea, a whale dives. A wolf runs for miles across a snow-covered plain. They fly, swim, and travel in search of food. Animals spend most of their time looking for a plant or animal to eat, which will nourish them, provide energy, or help their offspring survive. A food chain shows what living things in an area eat. Plants, called producers, are the first link

OPPOSITE: The plant-eating jackrabbit (which is a hare rather than a rabbit) uses its speed, senses, and coloring to avoid its many desert predators, including snakes, coyotes, and hawks.

on a food chain. Consumers, or animals that eat plants or other animals, make up the other links. The higher an animal is on the food chain, the less energy it receives from eating the animal below it. This is why there are more plants than plant eaters, and even fewer top consumers. Most animals eat more than one kind of plant or animal. Food webs show all of the possible food chains within a wildlife community.

With water shortages and hot and sometimes freezing temperatures, deserts are extreme environments for plants and animals to live within. Scientists categorize deserts, which take up about 20 percent of Earth's land surface, by the number of plants living in them and by their rainfall levels. Extreme deserts receive fewer than 3 inches (7.6 cm) of rainfall a year, and semi-deserts receive fewer than 15 inches (38.1 cm). In order to live in such a severe biome, plants and animals need special adaptations. More than 40 percent of the plants in a desert are annuals, which allows them to survive droughts as seeds. Many animals have adapted to deserts by hiding during the day and coming out only at night. Others have made physiological changes; some amphibians, for example, go dormant during the really hot times. The plants and animals in North American deserts make up numerous food chains, including one that begins with a tree and ends with a coyote.

Mesquite: Mighty Desert Plant

Hot deserts feature cacti, short plants, and areas with nothing but sand. Dunes, or hills of sand shaped by the wind, trap water for plants. Stony plains called regs are created in many deserts when wind blows away all the sand, leaving only pebbles or bare rock. Desert temperatures often soar above 122 °F (50 °C) during the day. Because of the dryness and lack of cloud cover at night, the temperature plummets after sunset, and the desert becomes cold. The extremes of heat in the day, cold at night, and a shortage of water at most times make survival nearly impossible for any human who comes to the desert unprepared.

When rain does come to the desert, it is often accompanied by violent storms, with fierce winds and lightning. Flash flooding is a common desert occurrence and happens when the rain falls so quickly that the sand cannot absorb it all, and the water rises. In the desert, it takes only about half a foot (15.2 cm) of water to carry off an object as heavy as a sport utility vehicle. Sometimes desert animals are killed in flash floods because they cannot get away or find shelter in time. Hikers and travelers can also suffer from the unpredictability of desert storms. Desert-goers have been driving or walking along without a raindrop falling or a gray cloud in the sky, when suddenly they were swept away by a river that seemed to come from nowhere. Unbeknownst to them, a storm had occurred miles away in another part of the desert.

What small amount of rain a desert receives depends upon its location in the world. Some years, a desert may get no rainfall, while other years it may experience triple the usual amount. The largest desert in the world is the Sahara in North Africa, which covers more than 3.3

Desert Cleaner

Even while circling in the sky for hours at a time, the turkey vulture does not have to flap its wings. Up and down with the air currents it soars, searching for carrion, or the rotting flesh of dead animals. As it lands on the hot sand, this huge bird with the six-foot (1.8 m) wingspan looks as if it is dressed for a funeral, with its black feathers and large black eyes. The turkey part of its name comes from the featherless, red-colored skin around its neck and face. Because turkey vultures prefer to feed on carrion, they play a key role in the desert food web. Without scavengers such as turkey vultures, dead animals would pile up, disease would spread, and the desert would reek of rot because decomposers such as bacteria could not break down the bodies fast enough. After the vulture finishes its feast of dead pronghorn or other animal carcass, small pieces of the dead animal's flesh or bones remain. However, these fragments do not go to waste. Bacteria inside maggots will break down what is left and return nutrients back to the soil, encouraging a new desert plant growth.

million square miles (8.5 million sq km). There are four smaller desert regions in North America, all located in the southwestern part of the United States and in Mexico. The Chihuahuan, Sonoran, and Mojave deserts have high temperatures and long summers. The Great Basin Desert is cooler and features different plant life, such as big sagebrush. After a good rain shower, a North American desert can look almost green, but this lasts only a short time. Plants such as cacti and the drought-tolerant mesquite tree are well-adapted to North American deserts and take maximum advantage of all the moisture they can find.

The mesquite tree is a phreatophyte, which means it has adapted to the desert by growing super-long roots to reach groundwater deep beneath the desert sand. Its roots have been found as far down as 175 feet (53.3 m), much deeper than the tree is tall. Outside the desert, the mesquite tree can grow to 50 feet (15.2 m) tall, but in the desert, it is similar to shrubs in size. Between the mesquite tree's leaves grow string-bean-sized pods with seeds. To help retain moisture and to protect new growth from foraging animals such as mule deer, a mesquite has thorns at the end of its young branch leaves. Up to three inches (7.6 cm) long, these thorns are strong enough to stab through shoes and tires.

The Cahuilla and Yuma Native American tribes used mesquite bark to make baskets, and Comanche

medicine men used mesquite leaves to treat illness. Cowboys found that mesquite made the best firewood because it was slow-burning and smokeless. The wood is also strong and today is used for furniture and fence posts. However, some people consider the tree a pest because it is difficult to remove once it has established itself, and it can grow back from a single strand of root.

The mesquite tree is an important food source for many desert animals and for humans as well. Tea and flour can be made from the tree's beans, and researchers have found that mesquite flour, despite its sweet taste, can control blood sugar in people with diabetes. Bees make a sweet-smelling honey from the tree's flowers, and many desert animals depend on mesquite seedpods for food. The coyote, one of the desert's top predators, is a carnivore, but when food is scarce, mesquite seedpods make up as much as 80 percent of its diet. Other animals, such as the Gambel's quail and Harris's antelope squirrel, regularly eat the hard, bean-sized seeds within the pods.

A mesquite tree also benefits when an animal eats one of its seeds. Sometimes a seed is not fully digested, and a day or two later, an animal deposits it in its waste in another location, spreading the mesquite tree's territory. A mesquite tree makes a lot of seeds, and each of them can survive as long as 40 years before sprouting. This leaves ample time for a ravenous herbivore to hop along and find it.

Merriam's Kangaroo Rat: Desert Hopper

The Merriam's kangaroo rat is not a kangaroo. And despite its name and appearance, it is not a rat either. It is, instead, closely related to squirrels. With teeth designed for gnawing, the kangaroo rat is a seedeater. As the smallest of the 22 North American kangaroo rat **species**, measuring 10 inches (25.4 cm), the Merriam's kangaroo rat's

Merriam's kangaroo rats try to avoid light as much as possible. They typically emerge from burrows only at night and will skip their nightly foraging if the moon is full.

short body could easily fit into a child's hand. Its six-inch (15.2 cm) tail makes up most of its size.

Adult kangaroo rats weigh about 1.4 ounces (40 g), or as much as a pair of shoelaces. With four toes on their overly large hind feet, they get around with bipedal movements.

Kangaroo rats can jump as far as six feet (1.8 m) at a time. Their long tail keeps them balanced while they jump and when they land. Covered in brownish fur that is lighter on their belly, they keep cool by staying in underground burrows

Mini-Monster

Reaching lengths of 21 inches (53.3 cm) and weighing as much as 3 pounds (1.4 kg), the Gila monster looks like a fat, pink, orange, and black snake with legs. Like snakes, Gilas flick their tongue, tasting and smelling the air for prey such as young desert tortoises, whose shells can be easily crushed and poisoned in a Gila monster's jaws. Using its strong claws, a Gila grips a young tortoise, clamps down its jaws, and injects venom from its 10 serrated lower teeth. Eating as much as half of its body weight at a meal, a Gila stores extra fat in its thick tail. In lean times, it is this fat that keeps the Gila alive, and it can survive for as long as a year off of what is stored in its tail. Gilas can live up to 20 years if they are not eaten by predators such as Harris's hawks. Partly because Gilas eat so many of the desert tortoise's young, this type of tortoise is now a threatened species.

during the day. When the scorching sun goes down, they come out of their den to look for food or find a mate. Male kangaroo rats are larger than females, and both are solitary animals until it comes time to have offspring. If there is a shortage of food, only a few females will breed.

The females are the sole providers for the babies and can have up to three litters a year, with an average of five born at a time. Newborn kangaroo rats come into the world hairless and helpless. The males in the litter grow faster than their sisters. The young rats start out crawling on all fours, but after two weeks, their large hind feet develop. Once their feet are large enough, the rats are ready to hop out of the den and start foraging for food.

One of the offspring usually takes over the mother's den after she dies, and the others find new homes. A kangaroo rat can live as long as five years, but it usually has a life expectancy of four months, due mainly to predators such as bobcats and kit foxes. A kangaroo rat's den is typically dug within 200 feet (61 m) of a food source, usually under a mesquite tree. It prefers sandy areas where it can easily make tunnels. Inside its den are many chambers used for sleeping or for storing food. During the hottest desert days, a kangaroo rat closes off its den with dirt. When desert storms come, the rat does not leave its home until the rain has passed. At night, when the temperature is cooler, it comes out to search

for seeds and insects and to defend its territory from intruding kangaroo rats. Each night, a kangaroo rat may hop across half an acre (0.2 ha) in search of seeds from the mesquite tree and creosote bush. Females will not venture as far if they have a nest.

A kangaroo rat takes sand baths by digging in the sand with its paws and rubbing its belly and side in the dirt. This helps it both cool off and spread its scent to let others know the boundaries of its territory. It also marks its territory with urine and feces. Thumping its feet on the ground, it will even attempt to scare away intruders such as coyotes. Out of its burrow, the kangaroo rat is most vulnerable, so it sometimes avoids coming out on nights with a full moon because the pale light may expose it to owls or other night predators.

A kangaroo rat's kidneys are well suited to handle a scarcity of water. The rat does not need to drink water, as it is able to get the moisture it needs just from seeds. Using both of its front limbs at the same time, it takes a kangaroo rat only a few seconds to store up to

Shelter and Sustenance

Despite the dry conditions of the Sonoran Desert in Arizona, California, and Mexico, some saguaro cacti live to be 200 years old. Saguaros can weigh as much as 2,000 pounds (907 kg) and reach heights of 50 feet (15.2 m). Two-inch (5.1 cm) thorns along their sides and branches help them conserve water. In May, the cacti bloom white flowers with yellow centers, providing **nectar** for desert insects such as bees and butterflies. In the fall, each piece of the saguaro's green fruit contains more than 4,000 seeds and serves as food for rodents, bats, and birds. The five-inch (12.7 cm) elf owl likes to live inside the giant saguaro and hunt for scorpions—**arthropods** with large, painful, and sometimes poisonous stingers—at night. The elf owl uses its strong beak to kill a scorpion and remove its stinger before flying back to the saguaro to eat. When the saguaro gets old and dies, termites will break the plant down into smaller pieces, bacteria will decompose the fragments, and nutrients will eventually be returned to the desert sand to help the next saguaro cactus grow.

60 seeds inside its fur-covered external cheek pouches, which are located beside its mouth. What it cannot carry in its pouches it scatter hoards. Scatter hoarding allows a kangaroo rat to quickly gather mesquite seeds, but it also makes it easy for other kangaroo rats or birds to steal from it. The mesquite piles are usually near a kangaroo rat's den, so it can easily reach and defend them.

Some kangaroo rats prefer to cache their mesquite seeds, storing them inside their dens for later use. Kangaroo rats do not usually eat their seeds until they are in the safety of their homes. If there is an area in the desert that contains many mesquite trees, a number of kangaroo rats will likely be nearby. In one desert study, as many as 95 percent of mesquite trees had a kangaroo rat den below them. And where there are kangaroo rats, not too far away there is almost certainly a sidewinding serpent in search of its own meal.

Sidewinder: Sneaky Slider

The sidewinder is a rattlesnake that is only about 32 inches (81.3 cm) long, but its venom has been known to kill people. Its fangs are as sharp as hospital needles, piercing fur and skin as they release shots of the snake's poison. The snake smells and tastes through a forked tongue and hears by vibrations picked up through its belly scales.

OPPOSITE: The sidewinder is sometimes referred to as the horned viper because of the raised scales over its eyes. These "horns" may help protect against blowing sand.

37

Sidewinder scales are rough to the touch and colored pink and gray, with blotches of brown and orange. With a life expectancy of about five years, a sidewinder grows a little each day, but its scales are not stretchable like human skin. Instead, it must shed its skin a couple of times a year to keep up with its growth. The rattle at the base of the sidewinder's tail is made of keratin, the same material as in human fingernails, and a new segment is added each time the snake sheds. When threatened, a

The rattle at the base of the sidewinder's tail is made of keratin, the same material as in human fingernails ...

sidewinder shakes its tail, which sounds like a baby's rattle, as a warning to other animals or people to stay away.

S idewinders mate between April and October. After the male and female mate, the rattlesnakes go their separate ways. The eggs stay inside the female until they hatch about 155 days later. Up to 18 young are born at a time. They have fangs and venom from birth and do not depend on their mother for protection.

When a sidewinder is young, it prefers small prey. Using a technique called caudal luring, which is similar to the method a fisherman uses in luring a fish with bait, a young sidewinder may shake its rattler to fool a small desert lizard. The lizard comes closer to the snake's rattler, thinking it is an insect, and within seconds, the young sidewinder has a meal. Most young sidewinders die within their first year, becoming part of the desert food web as they fall prey to king snakes or hawks. Those who survive soon reach adult size and become one of the desert's deadly predators.

Because sidewinders are reptiles, they have to regulate their body temperature externally. During the summer, sidewinders avoid the extreme midday heat by entering the burrow of another animal such as a desert pocket mouse; they may kill and eat the owner of the den if it is still there and then rest in the coolness found underground. The horns on a sidewinder's head get pressed

Desert Wasp

Despite its name, the tarantula hawk is neither a tarantula nor a hawk, but rather a wasp. Nine species of tarantula hawks live in the North American deserts. They are found wherever the large spiders called tarantulas make their homes. Two inches (5.1 cm) in length, the wasp has aposematic coloring, its orange wings warning other animals that messing with it might be a painful mistake. During the summer, tarantula hawks use their sense of smell to hunt for tarantulas. Once a tarantula has been located, the wasp stings it, paralyzing it. The wasp then drags the spider back to the spider's own den or to a new burrow in the sand that it has made just for the occasion and lays a single egg on the tarantula's abdomen. After sealing the den, the wasp leaves, and the tarantula is buried, paralyzed, for the rest of its life. When the wasp egg hatches, the baby wasp begins feeding on the still-living tarantula. Tarantula hawks have few predators, but roadrunners do eat them.

down and act like eyelids while the snake slithers through tight spaces, protecting its unblinking eyes from dirt.

The sidewinder moves across the desert sand in a sideways motion by applying a downward force in which only two parts of its body touch the sand. It is able to skip across the sand at speeds of three feet (91.4 cm) per second when in pursuit of such prey as a kangaroo rat or when escaping from a predator such as a bobcat. Scientists think sidewinders have adapted to moving sideways on the desert sand because the movement helps regulate

Mostly active at night, a sidewinder might travel as far as one mile (1.6 km) per night in search of food such as mice or kangaroo rats.

the snake's temperature. As the snake sidewinds, only a small percentage of its body comes into contact with the scorching sand during the day or the cold sand at night.

Mostly active at night, a sidewinder might travel as far as one mile (1.6 km) per night in search of food such as mice or kangaroo rats. A kangaroo rat is much too wary to fall for a rattlesnake's caudal luring, however. So, to catch a kangaroo rat, a sidewinder has to ambush it. Sometimes a sidewinder will slither into a kangaroo rat's den and, if it is not there, wait for it to return. Other times, it may bury itself under a mesquite tree and wait for the kangaroo rat to leave its den. Placing itself in a

Although many snake species have the ability to sidewind (over slick surfaces, for example), the sidewinder can travel at surprising speeds with this movement.

Located on the border of Arizona and Utah, Monument Valley is part of the Colorado Plateau, with steep, red-hued rock formations making up its desert landscape.

Roadrunner: Speed Racer

When American settlers started to move to the untamed West, they encountered a bird that could outrun their horse-drawn carriages and called it the roadrunner. Recognizable by its dark brown feathers streaked with white and its strong **zygodactyl feet**, a roadrunner can fly, but it prefers to run. Its legs seem to disappear on the desert sand as it reaches

... the roadrunner's wings are not strong enough to keep it off the ground for long; when it takes to the air, it can stay aloft for only a few seconds.

speeds as fast as 18 miles (29 km) per hour. Only in rare cases will the roadrunner choose to fly. When it is going downhill, it may opt to use its wings. It may also use them if it is startled by nearby danger. However, the roadrunner's wings are not strong enough to keep it off the ground for long; when it takes to the air, it can stay aloft for only a few seconds.

At a length of about two feet (61 cm), half of the road-runner's large size is its tail. The bird weighs about two pounds (0.9 kg), and its long beak and head are covered with spiked feathers in the shape of a crest. At the edge of each eye is a blue and orange featherless streak. The roadrunner has made adaptations to live in the desert. Before defecating, the roadrunner's body absorbs water from its feces, and a gland in its nose gets rid of extra salt.

Roadrunners make various sounds, including coos and preets, which are sweet music to a potential mate. A male roadrunner courts a female in the spring by bringing her a meal such as a scorpion. He bows his head low and lifts his wings. Fanning out his tail, he keeps it low to the sand and marches back and forth.

The strong-legged roadrunner is famously fast. However, despite the outcome shown in cartoons, a roadrunner cannot outrun a hungry coyote over long distances.

Roadrunners usually mate for the first time around two to three years of age and stay with their mates for life.

Roadrunners usually mate for the first time around two to three years of age and stay with their mates for life. Together, male and female roadrunners defend their territory and raise a family. They usually make their nest three feet (91 cm) off the ground in a clump of cacti or a mesquite tree, using shed snake skins, dung from horses, mesquite seedpods, feathers, and sticks. In May, the female lays 5 to 12 white-yellow eggs over a period of 3 days. The male does most of the incubating for the 20 days until the young hatch because, unlike the female, he can keep a constant body temperature through the night.

As the eggs hatch, both parents bring food to the young. Eggs in the nest that do not hatch are sometimes fed to the other young. If a predator such as a coyote comes near a roadrunner family, the male will crouch low, run away, and then stop. Standing tall and ruffling his head feathers up and down, he will turn his neck back and forth so that his colorful blue and orange eye streaks are visible. He will also make noises in an attempt to keep the predator's attention on him. Once the predator gives chase, the male runs for his life. If he outruns the threat, he will later return to the nest and continue his care of the young. After about 20 days, the baby roadrunners have grown the necessary feathers and can fly, and 2 weeks after that, they disperse. Roadrunners typically have a life expectancy of seven to eight years.

Roadrunner parents are very protective of their eggs and their hatchlings, but roadrunner families stay together for only about a month after the young are born.

The roadrunner was considered magical by some Native American tribes because of its strength and stamina against rattlesnakes. Its long tail and short wings help it maneuver the sharp turns necessary to both avoid the sidewinder's fangs and to chase the snake. When a hungry roadrunner spots a sidewinder, it runs to it and spreads its wings wide to block the snake's escape. Using its long, powerful beak and fighter plane speed, the bird grabs the sidewinder by its rattler and strikes the snake against the ground as if beating a dirty rug. Over and over, the roadrunner thrashes the snake, sometimes slamming it against a rock, cactus, or tree trunk. When it is satisfied that the snake is dead, the roadrunner swallows it whole.

Usually, the snake is too big for the roadrunner to ingest all at once, but this does not stop the bird. Hopping around the desert floor as if there is nothing long and limp hanging from its mouth, the roadrunner goes about its normal business. As part of the sidewinder is digested, the roadrunner stuffs more of the snake down its throat until eventually the whole snake is eaten. Even as it enjoys its snake snack, though, the roadrunner has to be wary of a prowling, four-legged enemy that can outrun even the speedy roadrunner.

Coyote: Desert Dog

At one time, coyotes were rare outside the American West. But where wolves were wiped out, coyotes moved in, and they now can be found all over North America. Male coyotes are larger and heavier than females and can be up to four feet (1.2 m) long, including their bushy tail. They look heavier than their average weight of 44 pounds (20 kg) because of thick fur that is reddish-brown everywhere except on their whitish throats and bellies.

OPPOSITE: Coyotes have shown that they can rapidly adapt to changing environments—even surviving in urban areas—with their only true predators being humans, cougars, and wolves.

Male coyotes sometimes court a female for up to three months before she decides on a partner.

In the desert, some coyotes live alone, but most live in packs of up to seven. Coyote packs consist of a mated pair, their offspring from former years, and recent pups. All members of the pack help in hunting and protecting the territory. They often search for food in relays, with the leader scouting for food such as mule deer or Harris's antelope squirrels. A coyote pack's territory may include as much as 12 square miles (31.1 sq km) of desert, and both males and females leave scent marks of urine all around it to make it known to other coyotes that this section of the land belongs to them.

Most coyotes are monogamous, which means they have one mate for life. In the pack, only one pair of coyotes breeds at a time. Male coyotes sometimes court a female for up to three months before she decides on a partner. A den is dug or taken over from another animal. Two months after coyotes mate, a litter of between 6 and 19 pups is born.

A mother coyote is very protective of her newborns. When the pups are three weeks old, they leave the den for the first time and go on short outings with their mother. To keep them in line, she uses a huffing sound when she wants them to return to her. The father

OPPOSITE Coyotes prefer to hunt or scavenge large prey, but in the desert, where options are limited, they often must settle for smaller targets such as roadrunners.

and the rest of the pack bring food to the mother and pups for several months. The pups first eat regurgitated food, moving to solid foods as they get older. At about seven weeks old, the pups no longer need their mother's milk, and at about four months of age, some of the young coyotes leave the pack.

There is a greater likelihood of death for the young coyote that decides to go it alone than for those that remain with the pack. Whether the coyote pups disperse or remain with their family, only about 12 percent of them will live

Although the coyote is not a particularly big animal, the harshness of the desert is not hospitable to larger carnivores, putting the coyote at the top of the food web.

past their first year. Even though an adult coyote is at the top of the desert food chain and can live up to 10 years, pups are much more vulnerable. Finding enough food is always a challenge, and sometimes disease kills them. Occasionally, adult coyotes from outside the pack will kill a pup. Humans also poison, trap, and shoot thousands of coyotes every year.

At sunset and sunrise, coyotes call to each other, their voices a mixture of yips, barks, and loud howls. It is often hard to judge how many coyotes might be calling to each

At sunset and sunrise, coyotes call to each other, their voices a mixture of yips, barks, and loud howls.

other because their voices can change several notes in a single call, making one coyote sound like four. These sounds are used to communicate where the coyotes are or to welcome or threaten other coyotes. Coyotes also communicate aggression, alertness, submissiveness, and other feelings by the positioning of their ears.

The coyote is an athletic animal and has been seen jumping over eight-foot (2.4 m) walls and even climbing tall chain-link fences to get to food. It can smell potential prey more than a mile (1.6 km) away, its hearing is acute, and it can detect the slightest movement in the sand. Running as fast as 29 miles (46.7 km) per hour, the coyote can usually catch whatever its nose, ears, and eyes have found. After the coyote has picked up the scent of a prey animal such as a roadrunner, it may stalk the animal for as long as 30 minutes before slowly getting closer.

When the roadrunner spots the approaching coyote, it begins running, and the coyote pursues in a sprint. The roadrunner may try to take to the air in a last-resort, desperate flight, but before it can, the swifter coyote clamps its jaws down, crushing the bird's fragile bones and organs. The coyote will eat the roadrunner's organs first and then its flesh, avoiding the feathers, beak, and talons unless it is really hungry.

The roadrunner in the coyote's belly is linked to the rattlesnake, the kangaroo rat, and the mesquite tree in the desert food chain. Scavengers, such as turkey vultures, will feed on the coyote's flesh after it dies, and bacteria will break down the fragments left behind. From the nutrients left in the sand, a new mesquite tree may take root, allowing the desert food chain to begin again.

Humpbacked Traveler

For thousands of years, camels have provided transportation for people who want to cross deserts. Camels have a high tolerance for heat. Their body temperature can rise as much as 11 °F (6.1 °C) above normal before they even begin to sweat. A camel can go without food or water for as long as seven days. In the desert, camels eat thorny shrubs, seeds, and dried-up leaves. They have even been known to eat canvas tents! Their eyelashes and the hairs in their ears are long to keep out sand, and their thick eyebrows act like the brim of a hat to block the sun. Camels have one or two humps made of fat. Reaching up to 7 feet (2.1 m) in height, camels can carry as much as 1,000 pounds (454 kg). In 1855, the U.S. decided to try using camels in the army after learning what great beasts of burden they were in the desert. When the Civil War broke out in 1861, more than 80 camels became the property of the Confederate Army. Humans also have historically used camels for milk, wool, and meat.

Selected Bibliography

Alsop, Fred J. III. *Smithsonian Handbooks: Birds of North America*. New York: DK, 2001.

Ernst, Carl H. *Venomous Reptiles of North America*. Washington, D.C.: Smithsonian Institution, 1992.

Faulk, Odie B. *The U.S. Camel Corps: An Army Experiment*. New York: Oxford University Press, 1976.

Lyttle, Richard B. *Birds of North America*. New York: Gallery Books, 1983.

Swinburne, Stephen R. *Coyote: North America's Dog*. Honesdale, Penn.: Boyds Mills Press, 1999.

Wilson, Don E., and Sue Ruff, eds. *The Smithsonian Book of North American Mammals*. Washington, D.C.: Smithsonian Institution, 1999.

Glossary

adaptations

changes an animal species makes over time—such as growing thicker fur or eating other foods—to survive in its environment

amphibians

cold-blooded animals that have a backbone; the young are gilled and live in the water, and adults breathe oxygen from the air; examples include frogs and newts

annuals

plants that grow for one season before dying in the winter

aposematic

describing an animal that has noticeable markings meant to warn other animals that eating it might result in illness or death

arthropods

animals, such as insects, that do not have backbones but have exoskeletons (hard outer shells), jointed legs, and segmented bodies

bacteria

microscopic, single-celled organisms that can live in the soil or water or inside animals and plants; some bacteria are helpful to their host, but others are harmful

biome

a region of the world that is differentiated from others by its predominant plant life and climate

bipedal

describing an animal that moves around by walking, hopping, or running on two feet

dormant	a state of reduced body activity in which an organism does not grow and its metabolism slows down
foraging	moving around in search of food
incubating	sitting on eggs so that the warmth will help the young inside develop until they are ready to hatch
nectar	a sweet liquid made by plants that is eaten by animals such as bees, butterflies, and hummingbirds
nutrients	minerals, vitamins, and other substances that provide an organism with what it needs to live, grow, and flourish
physiological	having to do with the growth, development, digestion, or other body processes of an organism at rest or during activity
predators	animals that live by killing for their food
regurgitated	partially digested food; some adult animals bring up partially digested food to feed their young
reptiles	cold-blooded animals that have a backbone and scaled skin or a hard shell; examples include snakes and turtles
scatter hoards	collects, piles, and stores seeds in different places; some animals gather food this way
scavengers	live animals that feed on dead animals

species	animals that have similar characteristics and are able to mate with each other
zygodactyl feet	feet in which two claws point forward and two point backward; examples include some kinds of birds such as the roadrunner

Index